John Stainer

A Choir-Book of the Office of Holy Communion

John Stainer

A Choir-Book of the Office of Holy Communion

ISBN/EAN: 9783337290016

Printed in Europe, USA, Canada, Australia, Japan

Cover: Foto ©Lupo / pixelio.de

More available books at **www.hansebooks.com**

A CHOIR BOOK

OF THE

Office of Holy Communion

FROM THE

CATHEDRAL PRAYER BOOK

EDITED BY

J. STAINER.

(PRICE ONE SHILLING AND SIXPENCE.)

LONDON : NOVELLO AND COMPANY, LIMITED.

NEW YORK · THE H. W. GRAY CO., SOLE AGENTS FOR THE U.S.A

MADE IN ENGLAND

SHORT SETTINGS

OF THE OFFICE FOR THE

HOLY COMMUNION

(INCLUDING *BENEDICTUS* AND *AGNUS DEI*

EXCEPT IN THOSE MARKED *)

FOR

PAROCHIAL AND GENERAL USE.

1. CALKIN, J. B., in C.
2. GARRETT, G. M., in A.
3. STAINER, J., in F.
4. ELVEY, G., in E.
5. TOURS, B., in C.
6. CRUICKSHANK, W. A. C., in E♭.
7. WOODWARD, H. H., in D.
8. HAYNES, B., in E♭.
9. HALL, K., in C.
10. †BRIDGE, J. F., in D.
11. BENNETT, G. J., in B♭.
12. *†LOHR H., in A minor.
13. †FIELD, J. T., in F.
14. †HALL, E. V., in C.
15. †CHAMPNEYS, F., in G.
16. *†WILLIAMS, C. L., in G.
17. †REDHEAD, A., in D.
18. †BLAIR, H., in F.
19. ALSOP, J. R., in E.
20. ILIFFE, F., in C.
21. ‡BLAIR, H., in G (*Men's Voices*).
22. STAMMERS, I. H., in E♭.
23. TOZER, F., in G (*Treble Voices*).
24. *ELLIOTT, J. W., in D.
25. †FISHER, A. C., in E♭.
26. FOSTER, M. B., in E♭.
27. NAYLOR, C. L., in D.
28. HALL, E. V., in E♭.
29. MARTIN, G. F, W., in E♭.
30. ROBERTS, J. V., in D.
31. HUGHES, P. E., in E.
32. †LIVETT, G. M., in G.
33. CARPENTER, T. L., in C

34. MARTIN, G. F. W., in E.
35. MARTIN, G. C., in C.
36. GODFREY, A. E., in E♭.
37. FOSTER, M. B., in C.
38. TOURS, F. E., in E♭.
39. STEGGALL, C., in A.
40. ROBERTS, J. V., in F (*Unison*).
41. TOZER, F., in F.
42. MOIR, F. L., in D.
43. PARKER, H., in B♭.
44. GODFREY, A. E., in F.
45. STEANE, B., in D.
46. EYRE, A. J., in E♭.
47. EYRE, A. J., in E and C.
48. WILLAN, H., in C and E♭.
49. HIGGS, H. M., in C.
50. PYNE, J. K., in A♭.
51. LEY, H. G., in B♭.
52. IRELAND, J., in C.
53. STOCKS, G., in F.
54. HOYTE, W. S., in D.
55. HALL, G. J., in D♭.
56. MARTIN, G. C., in A.
57. RHODES, H., in A.
58. ARMES, P., in A.
59. †ARMES, P., in B♭ (*Unison*).
60. ARMES, P., in G.
61. *STAINER, J., in C.
62. STEGGALL, R., in G.
63. MACPHERSON, C., in G.
64. FAULKES, W., in E.
65. WEST, JOHN E., in E♭.
66. O'CONNOR-MORRIS, G., in E♭.

ONE SHILLING AND SIXPENCE EACH

Except the numbers marked thus † which are now published in the Parish Choir Book Series, price One Shilling each ; and
‡ Now published in Men's Voice Series, No. 40, price One Shilling.

LONDON : NOVELLO AND COMPANY, LIMITED.

(July, 1923.)

A CHOIR BOOK

OF THE

Office of Holy Communion

FROM THE

CATHEDRAL PRAYER BOOK

EDITED BY

J. STAINER.

(PRICE ONE SHILLING AND SIXPENCE.)

LONDON : NOVELLO AND COMPANY, LIMITED.

NEW YORK · THE H. W. GRAY CO., SOLE AGENTS FOR THE U.S.A

MADE IN ENGLAND.

PREFACE.

The following account of the sources of the plain-song and other musical settings given in this Choir-book may be useful for reference.

The *Kyrie, Credo, Sanctus, Gloria, Agnus Dei, and Benedictus* are from Merbecke's Prayer-book of 1550, as reprinted cheaply by Messrs. Novello, under the editorship of Dr. Rimbault. But in all cases the notation of the Rev. T. Helmore has been adopted. No one who has ventured into the domain of plain-song can fail to express his indebtedness and gratitude to this accomplished musician for his labours in this branch of church music. The sources collated by Mr. Helmore are mentioned on p. 8 of his " Fuller Directory of the Plain-Song of the Holy Communion Service," a most valuable work which ought to be widely known.* The Editor is, however, responsible for the harmonisation of these and of all other melodies in this Choir-book.

The melody of the Confession is similar to the Lectionary Tone † and is taken from the ancient *Confiteor* (of the Pontifical Mass), as printed in Guidetti's *Directorium Chori*, Rome, 1624, *also* in Pustet's edition of the same work (Ratisbon, 1874); it will be found on p. 33 of the " Manual of Instructions on Plain Chant," by the Rev. James Jones, published in 1845; also on p. 157 of " Les vrais principes du Chant Grégorien," published at Malines in 1845. It is also given in the " Magister Choralis," by the Rev. Francis Xavier Haberl, p. 155. An interesting explanation of the notes intervening between the reciting-note and the final fall of a fifth in this form of the *Confiteor* may be read in Father Pothier's " Les Mélodies Grégoriennes," p. 262. It was sung (in conjunction with Helmore's version of Merbecke) for many years at the admirable choral services in Merton Chapel, Oxford, which, under the direction of the late Rev. Leighton George Hayne and the Rev. H. W. Sargent, kept alive the true spirit of Gregorian music; but the copies were only lithographed, and it was merely described as " ancient," no reference whatever being made to its source or authority.

Another simple form of *Lection* is illustrated by the melody of the sentences " Come unto me," &c., in which (after the usual fall and rise of a minor third

---

when stating the source of the words) there is uniformly a fall of a semitone for the comma, of a minor third for a semicolon, and of a fifth for the full stop. These sentences do not, as it happens, contain either a colon or a note of interrogation, otherwise they would be represented by the fall of a fourth, and by a semitone down and up respectively.

The melody of the *Sursum Corda* and *Prefaces* is to be found in almost every Missal with musical notes, including the Sarum Missal.

The *Lord's Prayer* is from Merbecke; the version here adopted (from Pickering's reprint) is given on p. 23 of Helmore's "Fuller Directory," where may be found other forms of the *Pater Noster*.

Space will not admit of any discussion on the exact relation between Merbecke's music and the ancient plain-song, but the reader is referred for some useful hints to the preface of Dyce's "Prayer Book with Plain Tune," published in 1843.

The extended *Amen, or Sevenfold Amen* given at the close of the *Prayer of Consecration* and after the *Blessing*, was composed by the editor expressly for use in St. Paul's Cathedral, when he was preparing this Choir-book at the request of the Dean and Chapter.

J. S.

6, AMEN COURT, *Easter*, 1883.

[It is hardly necessary to remind those to whom the training of choirs is entrusted, that strict time should be gradually relaxed as the singers become familiar with the text. The best rendering of plain-song is that which makes it follow the most natural recitation of the words, regardless of our modern notion as to the relative length of notes.— J. S. *Oxford*. 1895.]

THE ORDER FOR THE

ADMINISTRATION OF THE LORD'S SUPPER,

OR

HOLY COMMUNION.

¶ *So many as intend to be partakers of the holy Communion shall signify their names to the Curate, at least some time the day before.*

¶ *And if any of those be an open and notorious evil liver, or have done any wrong to his neighbours by word or deed, so that the Congregation be thereby offended; the Curate, having knowledge thereof, shall call him and advertise him, that in any wise he presume not to come to the Lord ι Table, until he hath openly declared himself to have truly repented and amended his former naughty life, that the Congregation may thereby be satisfied, which before were offended; and that he hath recompensed the parties, to whom he hath done wrong; or at least declare himself to be in full purpose so to do, as soon as he conveniently may.*

¶ *The same order shall the Curate use with those betwixt whom he perceiveth malice and hatred to reign; not suffering them to be partakers of the Lord's Table, until he know them to be reconciled. And if one of the parties so at variance be content to forgive from the bottom of his heart all that the other hath trespassed against him, and to make amends for that he himself hath offended; and the other party will not be persuaded to a godly unity, but remain still in his frowardness and malice: the Minister in that case ought to admit the penitent person to the holy Communion, and not him that is obstinate. Provided that every Minister so repelling any, as is specified in this, or the next precedent Paragraph of this Rubrick, shall be obliged to give an account of the same to the Ordinary within fourteen days after at the farthest. And the Ordinary shall proceed against the offending person according to the Canon.*

¶ *The Table, at the Communion-time having a fair white linen cloth upon it, shall stand in the Body of the Church, or in the Chancel, where Morning and Evening Prayer are appointed to be said. And the Priest standing at the North-side of the Table shall say the Lord's Prayer, with the Collect following, the people kneeling.*

OUR Father, which art in Heaven, Hallowed be thy Name. Thy kingdom come. Thy will be done in earth, As it is in heaven. Give us this day our daily bread. And forgive us our trespasses, As we forgive them that trespass against us. And lead us not into temptation; But deliver us from evil. Amen.

THE COLLECT.

ALMIGHTY God, unto whom all hearts be open, all desires known, and from whom no secrets are hid; Cleanse the thoughts of our hearts by the inspiration of thy Holy Spirit, that we may perfectly love thee, and worthily magnify thy Holy Name; through Christ our Lord.

A - men.

¶ *Then shall the Priest, turning to the people, rehearse distinctly all the TEN COMMANDMENTS; and the people still kneeling shall, after every Commandment, ask God mercy for their transgression thereof for the time past, and grace to keep the same for the time to come, as followeth.*

Minister.

GOD spake these words, and said; I am the Lord thy God: Thou shalt have none other Gods but me.

People.

Lord, have mer - cy up - on us, and incline our hearts to keep this law.

Lord, have mer - cy up - on us, and incline our hearts to keep this law.

Minister. Thou shalt not make to thyself any graven image, nor the likeness of any thing that is in heaven above, or in the earth beneath, or in the water under the earth. Thou shalt not bow down to them, nor worship them: for I the Lord thy God am a jealous God, and visit the sins of the fathers upon the children, unto the third and fourth generation of them that hate me, and shew mercy unto thousands in them that love me, and keep my commandments.

People. Lord, have mercy upon us, and incline our hearts to keep this law.

Minister. Thou shalt not take the Name of the Lord thy God in vain: for the Lord will not hold him guiltless, that taketh his Name in vain.

People. Lord, have mercy upon us, and incline our hearts to keep this law.

(2)

Minister. Remember that thou keep holy the Sabbath-day. Six days shalt thou labour, and do all that thou hast to do; but the seventh day is the Sabbath of the Lord thy God. In it thou shalt do no manner of work, thou, and thy son, and thy daughter, thy man-servant, and thy maid-servant, thy cattle, and the stranger that is within thy gates. For in six days the Lord made heaven and earth, the sea, and all that in them is, and rested the seventh day : wherefore the Lord blessed the seventh day, and hallowed it.

People. Lord, have mercy upon us, and incline our hearts to keep this law.

Minister. Honour thy father and thy mother; that thy days may be long in the land, which the Lord thy God giveth thee.

People. Lord, have mercy upon us, and incline our hearts to keep this law.

Minister. Thou shalt do no murder.

People. Lord, have mercy upon us, and incline our hearts to keep this law.

Minister. Thou shalt not commit adultery.

People. Lord, have mercy upon us, and incline our hearts to keep this law.

Minister. Thou shalt not steal.

People. Lord, have mercy upon us, and incline our hearts to keep this law.

Minister. Thou shalt not bear false witness against thy neighbour.

People. Lord, have mercy upon us, and incline our hearts to keep this law.

Minister. Thou shalt not covet thy neighbour's house, thou shalt not covet thy neighbour's wife, nor his servant, nor his maid, nor his ox, nor his ass, nor any thing that is his.

People.

Lord, have mer-cy up-on us, and write all these thy laws in our hearts, we be-seech thee.

¶ Then shall follow one of these two Collects for the King, the Priest standing as before, and saying,

Let us pray.

ALMIGHTY God, whose kingdom is everlasting, and power infinite; Have mercy upon the whole Church; and so rule the heart of thy chosen Servant *GEORGE*, our King and Governour, that he (knowing whose minister he is) may above all things seek thy honour and glory: and that we, and all his subjects (duly considering whose authority he hath) may faithfully serve, honour, and humbly obey him, in thee, and for thee, according to thy blessed Word and ordinance; through Jesus Christ our Lord, who with thee and the Holy Ghost liveth and reigneth, ever one God, world without end.

A - men.

Or,

ALMIGHTY and everlasting God, we are taught by thy holy Word, that the hearts of Kings are in thy rule and governance, and that thou dost dispose and turn them as it seemeth best to thy godly wisdom: We humbly beseech thee so to dispose and govern the heart of *GEORGE* thy Servant, our King and Governour, that, in all his thoughts, words, and works, he may ever seek thy honour and glory, and study to preserve thy people committed to his charge, in wealth, peace, and godliness: Grant this, O merciful Father, for thy dear Son's sake, Jesus Christ our Lord. *Amen.*

¶ Then shall be said the Collect of the Day.* And immediately after the Collect the Priest shall read the Epistle, saying, The Epistle [or, The portion of Scripture appointed for the Epistle] is written in the —— Chapter of —— beginning at the ——· Verse. And the Epistle ended, he shall say, Here endeth the Epistle. Then shall he read the Gospel (the people all standing up) saying, The holy Gospel is written in the —— Chapter of —— beginning at the —— Verse.

[¶ *The following is usually sung before the Gospel.*]

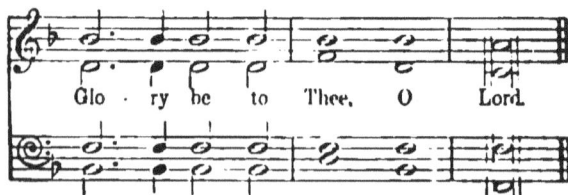

Glo - ry be to Thee, O Lord.

---

* For the proper Inflections of the Collect, Epistle, and Gospel, see p. 48.

[After the Gospel.]

Thanks be to Thee, O Lord.

¶ *And the Gospel ended, shall be sung or said the Creed following, the people still standing, as before.*

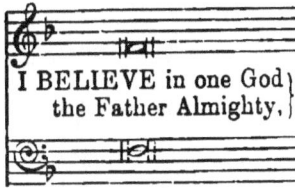

I BELIEVE in one God the Father Almighty, Maker of heaven and earth, And of all things visible and invisible:

And in one Lord Jesus Christ, the only begotten Son of God, Begotten of his Father before all worlds, God of God, Light of Light, Very God of very God, Begotten, not made, Being of one substance with the Father, By whom all things were made: Who for us men, and for our salvation came down from heaven, And was incarnate by the Holy Ghost of the Virgin Mary, And was made man, And was crucified also for us under Pontius Pilate. He suffered and was buried, And the third day he rose again according to the Scriptures, And ascended into heaven, And sitteth on the right hand of the Father. And he shall come again with glory to judge both the quick and the dead: Whose kingdom shall have no end.

And I believe in the Holy Ghost, The Lord and Giver of life, Who proceedeth from the Father and the Son, Who with the Father and the Son together is worshipped and glorified, Who spake by the Prophets. And I believe one Catholick and Apostolick Church. I acknowledge one Baptism for the remission of sins, And I look for the Resurrection of the dead, And the life of the world to come.

A - men

[Or this.]

Priest. FULL.

I BELIEVE in one God the Fa - ther Al - migh - ty,

Voices in Unison.

Org.

Ma-ker of heav'n and earth, And of all things vi - si - ble and in - vi - si-ble:

And in one Lord Je - sus Christ, the on - ly be-got - ten Son of God, Be -

- got - ten of his Fa - ther be - fore all worlds, God of God,

Light of Light, Ve - ry God of ve - ry God, Be - got - ten, not made.

(6)

Be - ing of one sub-stance with the Fa - ther ; By whom all things were

Faster. *Slow.*

made, Who for us men, and for our sal - va - tion came down from heaven.

p

Very soft and slow.

And was in - car - nate by the Ho - ly Ghost of the Vir - gin

Voices in Harmony, soft and slow.

And was in - car - nate by the Ho - ly Ghost of the Vir - gin

Ma - ry, And was made man, And was cru - ci - fi - ed al - so for us

Ma - ry, And was made man, And was cru - ci - fi - ed al - so for us

(7)

un - der Pon-ti-us Pi - late. He suf - fered and was bu - ri - ed.

un - der Pon-tius Pi - late. He suf - fered and was bu - ri - ed.

Quick.

And the third day he rose a-gain ac - cord- ing to the Scriptures, And as -

Voices in Unison, Quick.

- cen - ded in - to hea - ven, And sit - teth on the right hand of the

Fa-ther. And he shall come a-gain with glo - ry to judge both the quick and the dead · Whose king-dom shall have no end. And I be · lieve in the

Ho - ly Ghost, The Lord and Gi- ver of life, Who pro - ceed- eth from the

Fa - ther and the Son, Who with the Fa - ther and the Son to - gether is

wor · ship-ped and glo · ri -fied, Who spake by the Pro · phets. And

I be-lieve one Ca-tho-lick and A-pos-tolick Church. I ac-knowledge

one Bap-tism for the re-mis-sion of sins, And I look for the

Re-sur-rection of the dead, And the life of the world to come. A-men.

¶ *Then the Curate shall declare unto the people what Holy-days, or Fasting-days, are in the Week following to be observed. And then also (if occasion be) shall notice be given of the Communion : and the Banns of Matrimony published ; and Briefs, Citations, and Excommunications read. And nothing shall be proclaimed or published in the Church, during the time of Divine Service, but by the Minister : nor by him any thing, but what is prescribed in the Rules of this Book, or enjoined by the King, or by the Ordinary of the place.*

¶ *Then shall follow the Sermon, or one of the Homilies already set forth, or hereafter to be set forth, by authority.*

¶ *Then shall the Priest return to the Lord's Table, and begin the Offertory, saying one or more of these Sentences following, as he thinketh most convenient in his discretion.*

LET your light so shine before men, that they may see your good works, and glorify your Father which is in heaven. *St. Matth. v.*

Lay not up for yourselves treasure upon the earth; where the rust and moth doth corrupt, and where thieves break through and steal: but lay up for yourselves treasures in heaven; where neither rust nor moth doth corrupt, and where thieves do not break through and steal. *St. Matth.* vi.

Whatsoever ye would that men should do unto you, even so do unto them; for this is the Law and the Prophets. *St. Matth.* vii.

Not every one that saith unto me, Lord, Lord, shall enter into the Kingdom of heaven; but he that doeth the will of my Father which is in heaven. *St. Matth.* vii.

Zacchæus stood forth, and said unto the Lord, Behold, Lord, the half of my goods I give to the poor; and if I have done any wrong to any man, I restore four-fold. *St. Luke* xix.

Who goeth a warfare at any time of his own cost? Who planteth a vineyard, and eateth not of the fruit thereof? Or who feedeth a flock, and eateth not of the milk of the flock? 1 *Cor.* ix.

If we have sown unto you spiritual things, is it a great matter if we shall reap your worldly things? 1 *Cor.* ix.

Do ye not know, that they who minister about holy things live of the sacrifice; and they who wait at the altar are partakers with the altar? Even so hath the Lord also ordained, that they who preach the Gospel should live of the Gospel. 1 *Cor.* ix.

He that soweth little shall reap little; and he that soweth plenteously shall reap plenteously. Let every man do according as he is disposed in his heart, not grudgingly, or of necessity; for God loveth a cheerful giver. 2 *Cor.* ix.

Let him that is taught in the Word minister unto him that teacheth in all good things. Be not deceived, God is not mocked: for whatsoever a man soweth that shall he reap. *Gal.* vi.

While we have time, let us do good unto all men; and specially unto them that are of the household of faith. *Gal.* vi.

Godliness is great riches, if a man be content with that he hath: for we brought nothing into the world, neither may we carry any thing out. 1 *Tim.* vi.

Charge them who are rich in this world, that they be ready to give, and glad to distribute; laying up in store for themselves a good foundation against the time to come, that they may attain eternal life. 1 *Tim.* vi.

God is not unrighteous, that he will forget your works, and abour that proceedeth of love; which love ye have shewed for his Name's sake, who have ministered unto the saints, and yet do minister. *Hebr.* vi.

To do good, and to distribute, forget not; for with such sacrifices God is well pleased. *Hebr.* xiii.

Whoso hath this world's good, and seeth his brother have need, and shutteth up his compassion from him, how dwelleth the love of God in him ? 1 *St. John* iii.

Give alms of thy goods, and never turn thy face from any poor man ; and then the face of the Lord shall not be turned away from thee. *Tobit* iv.

Be merciful after thy power. If thou hast much, give plenteously : if thou hast little, do thy diligence gladly to give of that little : for so gatherest thou thyself a good reward in the day of necessity *Tobit* iv.

He that hath pity upon the poor lendeth unto the Lord : and look, what he layeth out, it shall be paid him again. *Prov.* xix.

Blessed be the man that provideth for the sick and needy : the Lord shall deliver him in the time of trouble. *Psal.* xli.

¶ *Whilst these Sentences are in reading, the Deacons, Churchwardens, or other fit person appointed for that purpose, shall receive the Alms for the Poor, and other devotions of the people, in a decent basin to be provided by the Parish for that purpose ; and reverently bring it to the Priest, who shall humbly present and place it upon the holy Table.*

¶ *And when there is a Communion, the Priest shall then place upon the Table so much Bread and Wine, as he shall think sufficient.*

Org.

After which done, the Priest shall say,

LET us pray for the whole state of Christ's Church militant here in earth.

ALMIGHTY and everliving God, who by thy holy Apostle hast taught us to make prayers, and supplications, and to give thanks, for all men ; We humbly beseech thee most mercifully
• *If there be no alms or oblations, then shall the words [of accepting our alms and oblations] be left out unsaid.* [*to accept our alms and oblations, and*] to receive these our prayers, which we offer unto thy Divine Majesty ; beseeching thee to inspire continually the universal Church with the spirit of truth, unity, and concord : And grant, that all they that do confess thy holy Name may agree in the truth of thy holy Word, and live in unity, and godly love. We beseech thee also to save and defend all Christian Kings, Princes, and Governours ; and specially thy Servant GEORGE our King ; that under him we may be godly and quietly governed : And grant unto his whole Council, and to all that are put in authority under him, that they may truly and indifferently minister justice, to the punishment of wickedness and vice, and to the maintenance of thy true religion and virtue. Give grace, O heavenly Father, to all Bishops and Curates, that they may both by their life and doctrine set forth thy true and lively Word, and rightly and duly administer thy holy Sacraments : And to all thy people give thy heavenly grace ; and

especially to this congregation here present; that, with meek heart and due reverence, they may hear, and receive thy holy Word; truly serving thee in holiness and righteousness all the days of their life. And we most humbly beseech thee of thy goodness, O Lord, to comfort and succour all them, who in this transitory life are in trouble, sorrow, need, sickness, or any other adversity. And we also bless thy holy Name for all thy servants departed this life in thy faith and fear; beseeching thee to give us grace so to follow their good examples, that with them we may be partakers of thy heavenly kingdom: Grant this, O Father, for Jesus Christ's sake, our only Mediator and Advocate.

A - men.

¶ *When the Minister giveth warning for the celebration of the holy Communion, (which he shall always do upon the Sunday, or some Holy-day, immediately preceding,) after the Sermon or Homily ended, he shall read this Exhortation following.*

DEARLY beloved, on —— day next I purpose, through God's assistance, to administer to all such as shall be religiously and devoutly disposed the most comfortable Sacrament of the Body and Blood of Christ; to be by them received in remembrance of his meritorious Cross and Passion; whereby alone we obtain remission of our sins, and are made partakers of the Kingdom of heaven. Wherefore it is our duty to render most humble and hearty thanks to Almighty God our heavenly Father, for that he hath given his Son our Saviour Jesus Christ, not only to die for us, but also to be our spiritual food and sustenance in that holy sacrament. Which being so divine and comfortable a thing to them who receive it worthily, and so dangerous to them that will presume to receive it unworthily; my duty is to exhort you in the mean season to consider the dignity of that holy mystery, and the great peril of the unworthy receiving thereof; and so to search and examine your own consciences, (and that not lightly, and after the manner of dissemblers with God; but so) that ye may come holy and clean to such a heavenly Feast, in the marriage-garment required by God in holy Scripture, and be received as worthy partakers of that holy Table.

The way and means thereto is; First, to examine your lives and conversations by the rule of God's commandments; and whereinsoever ye shall perceive yourselves to have offended, either by will, word, or deed, there to bewail your own sinfulness, and to confess yourselves to Almighty God, with full purpose of amendment of life. And if ye shall perceive your offences to be such as are not only against God, but also against your neighbours; then ye shall reconcile yourselves unto them; being ready to make restitution and satisfaction, according to the uttermost of your powers, for all injuries and wrongs done by you to any other; and being likewise ready to forgive others that have offended you, as ye would have forgiveness of your offences at God's hand: for otherwise the receiving of the holy Communion doth nothing else but increase your damnation. Therefore if any of you be a blasphemer of God an hinderer or slanderer of his Word, an adulterer, or be in malice, or envy, or in any other grievous crime, repent you of your sins, or else come not to that holy Table; lest, after the taking of that holy Sacrament, the devil enter into you, as he entered into Judas, and fill you full of all iniquities, and bring you to destruction both of body and soul.

And because it is requisite, that no man should come to the holy Communion, but with a full trust in God's mercy, and with a quiet conscience; therefore if there be any of you, who by this means cannot quiet his own conscience herein, but requireth further comfort or counsel, let him come to me, or to some other discreet and learned Minister of God's Word, and open his grief; that by the ministry of God's holy Word he may receive the benefit of absolution, together with ghostly counsel and advice, to the quieting of his conscience, and avoiding of all scruple and doubtfulness.

¶ Or, in case he shall see the people negligent to come to the holy Communion, instead of the former, he shall use this Exhortation.

DEARLY beloved brethren, on —— I intend, by God's grace, to celebrate the Lord's Supper: unto which, in God's behalf, I bid you all that are here present; and beseech you, for the Lord Jesus Christ's sake, that ye will not refuse to come thereto, being so lovingly called and bidden by God himself. Ye know how grievous and unkind a thing it is, when a man hath prepared a rich feast, decked his table with all kind of provision, so that there lacketh nothing but the guests to sit down; and yet they who are called (without any cause) most unthankfully refuse to come. Which of you in such a case would not be moved? Who would not think a great injury and wrong done unto him? Wherefore, most dearly beloved in Christ, take ye good heed, lest ye, withdrawing yourselves from this holy Supper, provoke God's indignation against you. It is an easy matter for a man to say, I will not communicate, because I am otherwise hindered with worldly business. But such excuses are not so easily accepted and allowed before God. If any man say, I am a grievous sinner, and therefore am afraid to come: wherefore then do ye not repent and amend? When God calleth you, are ye not ashamed to say ye will not come? When ye should return to God, will ye excuse yourselves, and say ye are not ready? Consider earnestly with yourselves how little such feigned excuses will avail before God. They that refused the feast in the Gospel, because they had bought a farm, or would try their yokes of oxen, or because they were married, were not so excused, but counted unworthy of the heavenly feast. I, for my part, shall be ready; and, according to mine Office, I bid you in the Name of God, I call you in Christ's behalf, I exhort you, as ye love your own salvation, that ye will be partakers of this holy Communion. And as the Son of God did vouchsafe to yield up his soul by death upon the Cross for your salvation; so it is your duty to receive the Communion in remembrance of the sacrifice of his death, as he himself hath commanded: which if ye shall neglect to do, consider with yourselves how great injury ye do unto God, and how sore punishment hangeth over your heads for the same; when ye wilfully abstain from the Lord's Table, and separate from your brethren, who come to feed on the banquet of that most heavenly food. These things if ye earnestly consider, ye will by God's grace return to a better mind: for the obtaining whereof we shall not cease to make our humble petitions unto Almighty God our heavenly Father.

¶ *At the time of the celebration of the Communion, the Communicants being conveniently placed for the receiving of the holy Sacrament, the Priest shall say this Exhortation.*

DEARLY beloved in the Lord, ye that mind to come to the holy Communion of the Body and Blood of our Saviour Christ, must consider how Saint Paul exhorteth all persons diligently to try and examine themselves, before they presume to eat of that Bread, and drink of that Cup. For as the benefit is great, if with a true penitent heart and lively faith we receive that holy Sacrament; (for then we spiritually eat the flesh of Christ, and drink his blood; then we dwell in Christ, and Christ in us; we are one with Christ, and Christ with us;) so is the danger great, if we receive the same unworthily. For then we are guilty of the Body and Blood of Christ our Saviour; we eat and drink our own damnation, not considering the Lord's Body; we kindle God's wrath against us; we provoke him to plague us with divers diseases, and sundry kinds of death. Judge therefore yourselves, brethren, that ye be not judged of the Lord; repent you truly for your sins past; have a lively and steadfast faith in Christ our Saviour; amend your lives, and be in perfect charity with all men; so shall ye be meet partakers of those holy mysteries. And above all things ye must give most humble and hearty thanks to God the Father, the Son, and the Holy Ghost, for the redemption of the world by the death and passion of our Saviour Christ, both God and man; who did humble himself, even to the death upon the

Cross, for us, miserable sinners, who lay in darkness and the shadow of death ; that he might make us the children of God, and exalt us to everlasting life. And to the end that we should alway remember the exceeding great love of our Master, and only Saviour, Jesus Christ, thus dying for us, and the innumerable benefits which by his precious blood-shedding he hath obtained to us ; he hath instituted and ordained holy mysteries, as pledges of his love, and for a continual remembrance of his death, to our great and endless comfort. To him therefore, with the Father and the Holy Ghost, let us give (as we are most bounden) continual thanks ; submitting ourselves wholly to his holy will and pleasure, and studying to serve him in true holiness and righteousness all the days of our life.

A - men.

¶ *Then shall the Priest say to them that come to receive the holy Communion,*

YE that do truly and earnestly repent you of your sins, and are in love and charity with your neighbours, and intend to lead a new life, following the commandments of God, and walking from henceforth in his holy ways ; Draw near with faith, and take this holy Sacrament to your comfort ; and make your humble confession to Almighty God, meekly kneeling upon your knees.

¶ *Then shall this general Confession be made, in the name of all those that are minded to receive the holy Communion, by one of the Ministers : both he and all the people kneeling humbly upon their knees, and saying,*

ALMIGHTY God, Father of our Lord Jesus Christ, Maker of all things, Judge of all men ; We acknowledge and bewail our manifold sins and wickedness, Which we, from time to time, most grievously have committed, By thought, word, and deed, Against thy Divine Majesty, Provoking most justly thy wrath and indignation against us. We do earnestly repent, And are heartily sorry for these our misdoings ; The remembrance of them is grievous unto us ; The burden of them is intolerable, Have mercy upon us, Have mercy upon us, most merciful Father ; For thy Son our Lord Jesus Christ's sake, Forgive us all that is past ; And grant that we may ever hereafter Serve and please thee In newness of life, To the honour and glory of thy Name ; Through Jesus Christ our Lord.

A - men.

[*Or this.*]

The Confession

WITH INFLECTIONS AND HARMONISED.

¶ Then shall this general Confession be made, all humbly kneeling upon their knees.

The Confession. (*Transposed.*)

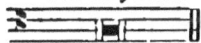

ALMIGHTY God,

Father of our Lord Je - sus Christ, Maker of all things,

Slow. (*Voices in Harmony.*)

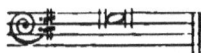

ALMIGHTY God,

Father of our Lord Je - sus Christ. Maker of all things,

Judge of all men ; We acknowledge and bewail our manifold sins and wick-edness.

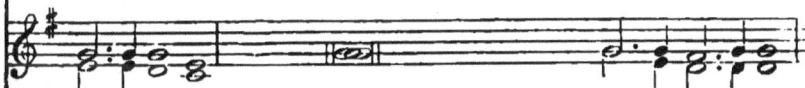

Judge of all men ; We acknowledge and bewail our manifold sins and wick-edness.

Which we, from time to time, most } grievously have committed,* by } thought, word, and deed,

Which we, from time to time, most } grievously have committed,* by } thought, word, and deed,

(17)

against Thy divine Ma - jes - ty, | Provoking most justly* Thy | -gainst us.
wrath and indignation a-

against Thy divine Ma - jes - ty, | Provoking most justly,* Thy | -gainst us.
wrath and indignation a-

We do earnestly repent,* and are | -do - ings ; | The remembrance | un - to us :
heartily sorry* for these our mis- | of them is grievous |

We do earnestly repent,* and are | -do - ings ; | The remembrance | un - to us ;
heartily sorry* for these our mis- | of them is grievous |

The burden of them is in-tolera-ble. Have mercy up-on us, Have mercy up-on us,

The burden of them is in-tolera-ble. Have mercy up-on us, Have mercy up on us,

Most merciful Fa-ther; { For Thy Son } Je-sus Christ's sake, { Forgive us } past ;
                        { our Lord } 　　　　　　　　　　 { all that is }

Most merciful Fa ther : { For Thy Son } Je-sus Christ's sake, { Forgive us } past ;
                         { our Lord } 　　　　　　　　　　　 { all that is }

And grant that we may ever hereafter serve and please Thee In new-ness of life,

And grant that we may ever hereafter serve and please Thee In new-ness of life,

To the honour and glory of Thy Name ; Thro' Je-sus Christ our Lord.　A-men.

To the honour and glory of Thy Name ; Thro' Je-sus Christ our Lord.　．A-men.

* *Then shall the Priest (or the Bishop, being present,) stand up, and turning himself to the people, pronounce this Absolution.*

ALMIGHTY God, our heavenly Father, who of his great mercy hath promised forgiveness of sins to all them that with hearty repentance and true faith turn unto him; Have mercy upon you; pardon and deliver you from all your sins; confirm and strengthen you in all goodness; and bring you to everlasting life; through Jesus Christ our Lord.

A - men.

* *Then shall the Priest say,*

* HEAR what comfortable words our Saviour Christ saith unto all that truly } turn to Him.

Organ. *

Hear what comfortable words our Saviour Christ saith unto all that truly } turn to Him.

St. Matth. xi. 28.

Come unto Me, all that travail and are } hea - vy la - den, and I will re - fresh you.

Come unto Me, all that travail and are } hea - vy la - den, and I will re - fresh you.

NOTE.—A soft combination of Steps on the Swell Organ should be used for the following accompaniments, and as a general rule the *Manual* only should be used, not the Pedal Organ. The Organist must, of course, be prepared to transpose the Organ Part to suit any pitch previously selected by the Minister.

So God lov-ed the world, that He gave His only be-got-ten Son,

So God loved the world, that He gave His only be-gotten Son,

St. John iii. 16.

to the end that all that believe in Him should not } per ish, but have everlasting life.

cres.

mf

to the end that all that believe in Him } should not per-ish, but have ever-last-ing life.

Hear al-so what Saint Paul saith. This is a true say-ing, { and worthy of all men to be re- }

p

Hear also what Saint Paul saith. This is a true say-ing, { and worthy of all men to } be re-

1 *Tim.* i. 15.

ceiv-ed, That Christ Jesus came into the world to save sin-ners.

-ceiv-ed. That Christ Jesus came into the world to save .. sin-ners.

Hear also what Saint John saith. If any man sin, we have an Advocate with the

Hear also what Saint John saith. If any man sin, we have an Advocate with the

1 *St. John* ii. 1.

Fa - ther, Jesus Christ the right-cous; and He is the propitiation for our sins

cres. *mf*

Fa ther, Jesus Christ the righteous; and He is the propiti-ation for our sins

Sursum Corda.

After which the Priest shall proceed, saying,

LIFT up your hearts.

Lift . up your hearts

Organ.

Answer.

We lift them up un - to the Lord.

We lift . . them up un - to the Lord. .

Priest.

LET us give thanks un - to our Lord God.

Let us give . . . thanks un - to . . our . . Lord God.

Answer.

It is meet and right so to do.

It is meet and right so to do. .

¶ *Then shall the Priest turn to the Lord's Table, and say,*

It is ve - ry meet, right, and our bound - en du - ty,

It is very meet. right, and our bound - en du - ty,

that we should at all times, and in all pla-ces, give thanks un - to Thee,

that we should at all times, and in all places, give thanks un - to Thee,

(23)

O Lord, *Ho-ly Fa-ther, Al-might-y, E-ver-last-ing God.

cres.

O Lord, *Holy Father, Almighty, Ever-last-ing God.

* These words [*Holy Father*] must be omitted on *Trinity Sunday.*

⸸ *Here shall follow the Proper Preface, according to the time, if there be any specially appointed : or else immediately shall follow,*

There-fore with Au-gels and Arch-an-gels, and with all the

p

There-fore with Angels and Arch-an-gels, and with all the

com-pa-ny of heaven we laud and magni-fy Thy glo-ri-ous Name;

cres.

com-pa-ny of heaven we laud and magnify Thy glo-rious Name;

e-ver-more prais-ing Thee, and say-ing,

mf

e-ver-more prais-ing Thee, and say-ing,

Sanctus.

Ho - ly, Ho - ly, Ho - ly, Lord God of Hosts, Heaven and earth are

Organ copy, transposed.
Voices in Unison (not Harmony).*

Ho - ly, Ho - ly, Ho - ly, Lord God of Hosts, Heaven and earth are

full of Thy Glo - ry: Glo - ry be to Thee, O Lord most High. A - men.

full of Thy Glo - ry: Glo - ry be to Thee, O Lord most High. A - men.

or this: (see Footnote.)

Voices in Harmony (or Unison).

Ho - ly, Ho - ly, Ho - ly, Lord God of Hosts, Heaven and earth are

full of Thy Glo - ry: Glo - ry be to Thee, O Lord most High. A - men.

* NOTE.—When the *Sursum Corda*, &c., are sung in the key of E flat, the *Sanctus* should be sung in Unison in B flat; when the former is sung in G, the latter should be in G also.

(35)

Proper Prefaces.

Upon CHRISTMAS DAY, and seven days after

Be - cause Thou didst give Je - sus Christ Thine On - ly Son

Be - cause Thou didst give Je - sus Christ Thine On - ly Son

to be born as at this time for us; Who, by the o - per - a - tion

to be born as at this time. . for us; Who, by the oper - ation

of the Ho - ly Ghost, was made ve - ry man of the sub - stance of the

of the Ho - ly Ghost, was made ve - ry man of the sub - stance of the

Vir - gin Ma - ry His Mo - ther; and that without spot of sin,

Vir - gin Ma - ry His Mo - ther; and that without spot of sin,

to make us clean from all sin. There-fore with An-gels, &c.
dim.

to make us clean from . . all sin. There-fore with Angels, &c.

Upon EASTER DAY, *and seven days after.*

But chiefly are we bound to praise Thee for the glo-ri-ous Resurrection of Thy
p
cres.

But chiefly are we bound to praise Thee for the glorious Re-sur-rection of Thy

Son Je - sus Christ our Lord: for He is the ve-ry Pas-chal
dim.
p

Son Je - sus Christ our Lord: for He is the ve-ry Pas-chal

Lamb, which was of-fer-ed for us, and hath ta-ken a-way
dim.
pp

Lamb, which was offer-ed for . . us, . . and hath ta-ken a-way

(27)

the sin of the world; Who by His death hath de - cres.

the sin .. of .. the .. world; .. Who by His death hath de .

stroy - ed death, and by His ris-ing to life again hath restored to

- stroy - ed death, and by .. His rising to life again hath restored to

us e - ver - last - ing life. There - fore with An - gels, &c.

us . e - ver - last - ing life. There - fore with Angels, &c.

Upon ASCENSION DAY, *and seven days after.*

Through Thy most dear- ly be - lov - ed Son Je - sus Christ

Through Thy .. most dearly be - lov - ed Son Je - sus Christ

(28)

our Lord ; Who af-ter His most glo-ri-ous Resurrection man-i-fest-ly up-
ores.

our . . Lord ; Who after His most glorious Resurrection manifestly ap-

pear-ed to all His A - pos - tles, and in their sight as-

- peared to all His A - - pos - tles, and in their sight as-

- cend-ed up in - to heaven to pre-pare a place

- cend-ed up in - to heaven to pre-pare a . . place . .

for us ; that where He is, thi-ther we might al - so as-cend,
dim.

for . . us ; that where He is, thither we might al - so ascend, and reign with Him in glo - ry. There - fore with An-gels, &c.

cres.

and reign with Him in glo - ry. There - fore with Angels, &c.

Upon WHITSUNDAY, *and six days after.*

Through Je - sus Christ our Lord; ac-cord-ing to Whose

Through Je - sus . . Christ . . . our . . Lord; ac - cording to Whose

most true pro - mise, the Ho-ly Ghost came down as at this time from

most true . . pro - mise, the Holy Ghost came down as at this time from

Heaven with a sud - den great sound, as it had been a migh - ty wind,

cres.

Heaven with a sud - den great sound, as it had been a . . migh-ty wind, in the likeness of fi - e -ry tongues, lighting upon the Apostles, to teach them,

in the likeness of fiery tongues, lighting upon the A-postles, to teach them,

and to lead them to all truth; giv-ing them both the

dim.

and to lead them to . . . . all . . truth; giv-ing them both the

gift of di - vers lan - gua-ges, and al - so boldness with fervent zeal

cres.

gift of di - vers lan - gua-ges, and also boldness with fervent zeal

con-stant-ly to preach the Gos-pel un to all na tions;

constantly to preach the Gos - pel un - to . . all na tions;

where-by we have been brought out of dark-ness and er - ror

where - by we have been brought out of darkness and . . er - ror

in - to the clear light and true knowledge of Thee, and of Thy

mf

in - to the clear light and true knowledge of Thee, . . and of Thy . .

Son Je - sus Christ. There fore with An-gels, *&c.*

Son . . Je - sus Christ. There - fore with Angels, *&c.*

Upon the Feast of TRINITY *only.*

Who art one God. one Lord ; not one

Who art one God, one . . Lord ; . . not one

or - ly Per - son, but three Per-sons in one

on - ly Per - son, but three Per-sons in . one . .

Sub-stance. For that which we be-lieve of the glo - ry of the Fa - ther,

cres.

Sub- stance. For that which we believe of the glory of the Fa - ther,

the same we be-lieve of the Son, and of the Ho- ly Ghost, without a - ny

dim.

the same we be-lieve of . . the Son, and of the Ho- ly Ghost, without any

dif - fer-ence or in - e - qual - i - ty. There - fore with An-gels, &c

dif- fer-ence or . . in - e - qual - i - ty. There- fore with Angels, &c.

¶ After each of which Prefaces shall immediately be sung or said,

THEREFORE with Angels and Archangels, and with all the company of heaven, we laud and magnify thy glorious Name; evermore praising thee, and saying, Holy, holy, holy, Lord God of hosts, heaven and earth are full of thy glory : Glory be to thee, O Lord most High. *Amen.*

¶ Then shall the Priest, kneeling down at the Lord's Table, say in the name of all them that shall receive the Communion this Prayer following.

Org.

WE do not presume to come to this thy Table, O merciful Lord, trusting in our own righteousness, but in thy manifold and great mercies. We are not worthy so much as to gather up the crumbs under thy Table. But thou art the same Lord, whose property is always to have mercy : Grant us therefore, gracious Lord, so to eat the flesh of thy dear Son Jesus Christ, and to drink his blood, that our sinful bodies may be made clean by his body, and our souls washed through his most precious blood, and that we may evermore dwell in him, and he in us.

A - men.

Benedictus.

(AFTER MERBECKE.)

Bless-ed is He that com-eth in the Name of the Lord. Ho

Moderato.

Bless - ed is He that com -eth in the Name of the Lord. Ho -

san·na in the highest.

Allegro.

san·na in the high·est, Ho san·na in the high est.

Tempo primo.

Bless·ed is He that com·eth in the Name of the Lord. Ho

Allegro.

san·na in the high·est, Ho·san·na in the high·est, the

high est, Ho·san·na in the high est.

The Consecration.

¶ *When the Priest, standing before the Table, hath so ordered the Bread and*
Wine, that he may with the more readiness and decency break the Bread
before the people, and take the Cup into his hands, he shall say the Prayer
of Consecration, as followeth.

ALMIGHTY God, our heavenly Father, who of thy
tender mercy didst give thine only Son Jesus Christ to

suffer death upon the cross for our redemption ; who made there (by his one oblation of himself once offered) a full, perfect, and sufficient sacrifice, oblation, and satisfaction, for the sins of the whole world ; and did institute, and in his holy Gospel command us to continue, a perpetual memory of that his precious death, until his coming again ; Hear us, O merciful Father, we most humbly beseech thee ; and grant that we receiving these thy creatures of bread and wine, according to thy Son our Saviour Jesus Christ's holy institution, in remembrance of his death and passion, may be partakers of his most blessed Body and Blood : who, in the same night that he was betrayed, *took Bread ; and when he had given thanks, †he brake it, and gave it to his disciples, saying, Take, eat, ‡this is my Body which is given for you : Do this in remembrance of me. Likewise after supper he ‖took the Cup ; and, when he had given thanks, he gave it to them, saying, Drink ye all of this ; for this §is my Blood of the New Testament, which is shed for you and for many for the remission of sins : Do this, as oft as ye shall drink it, in remembrance of me.

* Here the Priest is to take the Paten into his hands :

† And here to break the Bread :

‡ And here to lay his hand upon all the Bread.

‖ Here he is to take the Cup into his hand :

§ And here to lay his hand upon every vessel (be it Chalice or Flagon) in which there is any Wine to be consecrated.

A - men.

[Or this.]

J. STAINER (Oct. 1873).

Slow and sustained. cres. A - men, A

A - men, A - men, A

A - men, A

men, dim. A men, Slower.

men, A men, A men, A men.

men, A men, A men, A men.

Agnus Dei.

(AFTER MERBECKE.)

O Lamb of God, that ta - kest a - way the

O Lamb of God, that ta - kest a - way the

sins of the world, have mer cy up - on us.

sins of the world, have mer - cy up - on us.

A short Interlude on the Organ.

O Lamb of God, that ta - kest a - way tho

O Lamb of God, that ta - kest a - way the

sins of the world, have mer · cy up · on us.

sins of the world. have mer - cy up on us.

A short Interlude on the Organ.

O Lamb of God, that ta kest a · way the

O Lamb of God, that ta · kest a way the

sins of the world, grant us thy peace.

Slow.

sins of the world, grant us thy peace.

(38)

⁋ *Then shall the Minister first receive the Communion in both kinds himself, and then proceed to deliver the same to the Bishops, Priests, and Deacons, in like manner, (if any be present,) and after that to the people also in order, into their hands, all meekly kneeling. And, when he delivereth the Bread to any one, he shall say,*

THE Body of our Lord Jesus Christ, which was given for thee, preserve thy body and soul unto everlasting life. Take and eat this in remembrance that Christ died for thee, and feed on him in thy heart by faith with thanksgiving.

⁋ *And the Minister that delivereth the Cup to any one shall say,*

THE Blood of our Lord Jesus Christ, which was shed for thee, preserve thy body and soul unto everlasting life. Drink this in remembrance that Christ's Blood was shed for thee, and be thankful.

[A Hymn may be sung, or the Organ may be played softly while the Clergy and People receive the Communion.]

⁋ *If the consecrated Bread or Wine be all spent before all have communicated, the Priest is to consecrate more according to the Form before prescribed, beginning at* [Our Saviour Christ in the same night, &c.] *for the blessing of the Bread; and at* [Likewise after Supper, &c.] *for the blessing of the Cup.*

⁋ *When all have communicated, the Minister shall return to the Lord's Table, and reverently place upon it what remaineth of the consecrated Elements, covering the same with a fair linen cloth.*

⁋ *Then shall the Priest say the Lord's Prayer, the people repeating after him every Petition.*

OUR Father, which art in heaven, Hallowed be thy Name. Thy kingdom come. Thy will be done in earth, As it is in heaven. Give us this day our daily bread. And forgive us our trespasses, As we forgive them that trespass against us. And lead us not into temptation : But deliver us from evil : For thine is the kingdom. The power, and the glory, For ever and ever. A - men.

[*Or this.*]

Priest.   **People.** *Slow and sustained.*

Our Father,   which art in heaven, Hal-low-ed be thy Name.

Slow and sustained.   *pp*

Org.
Our Father.   which art in heaven, Hal-low-ed be thy Name.

Thy king-dom come. Thy will be done in earth, As it is in heaven:

Thy king-dom come. Thy will be done in earth, As it is in heaven:

Give us this day our dai-ly bread. And for-give us our tres-pass-es,

Give us this day our dai-ly bread. And for-give us our tres-pass-es,

As we for-give them that tres-pass a-gainst us. And lead us not

As we for-give them that tres-pass a-gainst us. And lead us not

in - to temp-ta - tion; But de - li - ver us from e vil : For thine is
pp *rall.*

in - to temp-ta - tion; But de - li - ver us from e - vil : For thine is

the king-dom, The power, and the glo - ry, For e - ver and e - ver. A - men.
dim. *pp slow.*

the king-dom, The power, and the glo - ry, For e - ver and e - ver. A - men.

¶ *After shall be said as followeth.*

O LORD and heavenly Father, we thy humble servants entirely desire thy fatherly goodness mercifully to accept this our sacrifice of praise and thanksgiving; most humbly beseeching thee to grant, that by the merits and death of thy Son Jesus Christ, and through faith in his blood, we and all thy whole Church may obtain remission of our sins, and all other benefits of his passion. And here we offer and present unto thee, O Lord, ourselves, our souls and bodies, to be a reasonable, holy, and lively sacrifice unto thee; humbly beseeching thee, that all we, who are partakers of this holy Communion, may be fulfilled with thy grace and heavenly benediction. And although we be unworthy, through our manifold sins, to offer unto thee any sacrifice, yet we beseech thee to accept this our bounden duty and service: not weighing our merits, but pardoning our offences, through Jesus Christ our Lord; by whom, and with whom, in the unity of the Holy Ghost, all honour and glory be unto thee, O Father Almighty, world without end.

A - men.

Or this.

ALMIGHTY and everliving God, we most heartily thank thee, for that thou dost vouchsafe to feed us, who have duly received these holy mysteries, with the spiritual food of the most precious Body and Blood of thy Son our Saviour Jesus Christ; and dost assure us thereby of thy favour and goodness towards us; and that we are very members incorporate in the mystical body of thy Son, which is the blessed company of all faithful people; and are also heirs through hope of thy everlasting kingdom, by the merits of the most precious death and passion of thy dear Son. And we most humbly beseech thee, O heavenly Father, so to assist us with thy grace, that we may continue in that holy fellowship, and do all such good works as thou hast prepared for us to walk in; through Jesus Christ our Lord, to whom, with thee and the Holy Ghost, be all honour and glory, world without end.

A - men.

¶ *Then shall be said or sung,*

GLORY be to God on high,

and in earth peace, good will towards men. We praise thee, we bless thee, we worship thee, we glorify thee, we give thanks to thee for thy great glory, O Lord God, heavenly King, God the Father Almighty.

O Lord, the only begotten Son Jesu Christ; O Lord God, Lamb of God, Son of the Father, that takest away the sins of the world, have mercy upon us. Thou that takest away the sins of the world, have mercy upon us. Thou that takest away the sins of the world, receive our prayer. Thou that sittest at the right hand of God the Father, have mercy upon us.

For thou only art holy; thou only art the Lord; thou only, O Christ, with the Holy Ghost, art most high in the glory of God the Father.

A - men.

Priest. [*Or this.*]

Glo - ry be to God on high, and in earth

Org.

Glo - ry be to God on high, and in earth

(42)

peace, good will towards men. We praise thee, we bless thee, wo

peace, good will towards men. We praise thee, we bless thee, we

wor - ship thee, we glo-ri-fy thee, we give thanks to thee for thy great

wor-ship thee, we glo-ri-fy thee, we give thanks to thee for thy great

glo - ry, O Lord God, heaven - ly King, God the Fa - ther Al -

glo - ry, O Lord God, heaven-ly King, God the Fa - ther Al -

- nigh - ty. O Lord, the on - ly be-got-ten Son Je - su Christ;

- migh - ty. O Lord, the on - ly be-got - ten Son Je - su Christ;

O Lord God, Lamb of God, Son of the Fa - ther, that
O Lord God, Lamb of God, Son of the Fa - ther, that

ta - kest a way the sins of the world, have mer - cy up -
ta - kest a-way the sins of the world, have mer - cy up -

- on us. Thou that ta - kest a-way the sins of the world, have
- on us. Thou that ta - kest a-way the sins of the world, have

mer - cy up - on us. Thou that ta - kest a-way the sins of the world, re -
mer - cy up - on us. Thou that ta - kest a-way the sins of the world, re -

ceive our prayer. Thou that sit-test at the right hand of God the Fa - ther, have mer-cy up-on us. For thou on-ly art ho - ly; thou on-ly art the Lord; thou on-ly, O Christ, with the Ho-ly Ghost, art most high in the glo-ry of God the Fa-ther. A - men.

¶ Then the Priest (or Bishop if he be present) shall let them depart with this Blessing.

Org.

THE peace of God, which passeth all understanding, keep your hearts and minds in the knowledge and love of God, and of his Son Jesus Christ our Lord : and the blessing of God Almighty, the Father, the Son, and the Holy Ghost, be amongst you and remain with you always.

A - men.

[Or this.]

Org.

THE peace of God, which passeth all understanding, keep your hearts and minds in the knowledge and love of God, and of his Son Jesus Christ our Lord, and the bless-ing of God Al-migh-ty, the Fa-ther, the Son, and the Ho-ly Ghost, be amongst you, and remain with you al-ways.

Slow and sustained. cres. A · men, A · · · · · ·

A men. A · men, A

pp cres.

A

men, f dim. pp A · · · men, Slower. ppp

men, A men, A men. A · men.

A f dim. pp ppp

men, f men, A men, A · men.

¶ *Collects to be said after the Offertory, when there is no Communion, every such day one or more; and the same may be said also, as often as occasion shall serve, after the Collects either of Morning or Evening Prayer, Communion, or Litany, by the discretion of the Minister.*

ASSIST us mercifully, O Lord, in these our supplications and prayers, and dispose the way of thy servants towards the attainment of everlasting salvation; that, among all the changes and chances of this mortal life, they may ever be defended by thy most gracious and ready help; through Jesus Christ our Lord. *Amen.*

O ALMIGHTY Lord, and everlasting God, vouchsafe, we beseech thee, to direct, sanctify, and govern, both our hearts and bodies, in the ways of thy laws, and in the works of thy commandments; that through thy most mighty protection, both here and ever, we may be preserved in body and soul; through our Lord and Saviour Jesus Christ. *Amen.*

GRANT, we beseech thee, Almighty God, that the words, which we have heard this day with our outward ears, may through thy grace be so grafted inwardly in our hearts, that they may bring forth in us the fruit of good living, to the honour and praise of thy Name; through Jesus Christ our Lord. *Amen.*

PREVENT us, O Lord, in all our doings with thy most gracious favour, and further us with thy continual help; that in all our works begun, continued, and ended in thee, we may glorify thy holy Name, and finally by thy mercy obtain everlasting life; through Jesus Christ our Lord. *Amen.*

ALMIGHTY God, the fountain of all wisdom, who knowest our necessities before we ask, and our ignorance in asking; We beseech thee to have compassion upon our infirmities; and those things, which for our unworthiness we dare not, and for our blindness we cannot ask, vouchsafe to give us, for the worthiness of thy Son Jesus Christ our Lord. *Amen.*

ALMIGHTY God, who hast promised to hear the petitions of them, that ask in thy Son's Name; We beseech thee mercifully to incline thine ears to us that have made now our prayers and supplications unto thee; and grant, that those things, which we have faithfully asked according to thy will, may effectually be obtained, to the relief of our necessity, and to the setting forth of thy glory; through Jesus Christ our Lord. *Amen.*

The Tones for the Collect, Epistle, and Gospel.*

THE COLLECTS.

THE Festival Tone is used at Mattins, Evensong, and celebration of the Holy Communion on all Sundays, Holy-days, and Commemorations.

In the example given, it will be observed that there are two inflections; the first, Fa, Mi, Re, Fa, called the Punctum Principale; the second, Fa, Mi, called the Semipunctum. Care must be taken that the Collect itself, or the body of the Collect, be distinguished from the conclusion. The Collect generally consists of two, three, or more members; but whatever number of members there may be, the Punctum and Semipunctum are only used *once* each in the same Collect, and *once* in the conclusion of the Collect.

At the end of the first member or clause the Punctum is placed; the Semipunctum closes the second member, which frequently begins with the word "Grant," or "Grant, we beseech Thee." If the Collect concludes with "Through Jesus Christ our Lord," *e.g.*, Collect for Ash Wednesday,† or with, "Who livest and reignest" (without "Through Jesus Christ"), *e.g.*, first Sunday in Lent,‡ the Semipunctum is omitted, and the Punctum only is used.

Al-might·y God, Who hast giv·en us Thy on·ly be·got·ten

Son to take our na·ture up·on Him, and as at this time to be
(*Punctum Principale.*) (*Semipunctum.*)

born of a pure Vir·gin; Grant that we be·ing re·ge·ne·rate,
(*Semipunctum.*)

and made Thy children ... through the same our Lord Jesus Christ, Who liv·eth and reigneth
(*Punctum Principale.*)

with Thee and the same Spi·rit, e·ver one God, world with·out end. A·men.

* By the kind permission of the Rev. Henry Aston Walker, M.A., these Rules are quoted from his Manual for the Holy Communion (Novello).

† *Conclusion of Collect for Ash Wednesday, an example of the Semipunctum being omitted.*

(*Punctum Principale.*)

Through Je - sus Christ our Lord.   A - men.

‡ *Conclusion of Collect for 1st Sunday in Lent, shewing the Semipunctum omitted.*

(*Punctum Principale.*)

honour and glory, Who liv-est and reign-est with the Fa-ther and the Ho-ly

Ghost, one God,   world with-out end.   A - men.

The Ferial Tone is used on Simples and Ferias, and at Burials, and has no inflections: the Collect is sung on one note throughout, *e.g.*, Fa. However, there is an inflection allowed on Ferias when many prayers have been said, *e.g.*, at the last prayer of Mattins, Evensong, and the Litany. It is on the penultimate syllable from Fa to Re.

THE EPISTLE.

The Epistle is sung on one note, *e.g.*, Fa.* There is an inflection, when an interrogation occurs, *e.g.*, Epistle for Christmas Day.

Thou art my Son, this day have I be-got-ten Thee? And a-gain,

I will be to Him a Fa-ther, and He shall be to me a Son.

The fourth syllable before a period is much prolonged, *e.g.*—

And let all the an-gels of God wor-ship Him.

And an inflection on the fourth syllable, or nearest important to that from the end, *e.g.*—

But thou art the same, and Thy years shall not fail.

* In the Manual from which these Rules are quoted the Clef for the Epistle and Gospel is as C.

THE GOSPEL.

The Gospel admits of an inflection from the dominant to a third below, *e.g.*, Fa to Re, on the fourth* syllable from a period.† Also before an interrogation, as in the Epistle, and on the fifth syllable from the end,‡ as *e.g.*, in the Gospel for Christmas Day.

The Holy Gospel is written in the First Chapter of the Holy Gospel according to Saint John.

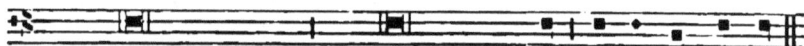

† In the beginning was the Word, and the Word was with God, and the Word was God.

The same was in the beginning with God.　｛All things were made by Him; and without Him was not｝

a-nything made that was made. . . ｛of the Fa-ther, full of grace and truth.

---

* This rule cannot always be rigidly kept; when not, the inflection should be made on the most important word or syllable of a word nearest the fourth

PUBLISHED AS NET BOOKS.

THE CATHEDRAL PRAYER BOOK
AND
CATHEDRAL PSALTER
(FOR USE OF THE WELSH CHURCH).

EDITED BY
THE REV. W. WILLIAMS, B.D.
(Canon Residentiary and Vicar of St. David's)
AND
T. EDWARDS
(Chester).

STAFF NOTATION EDITIONS.

No.		s.	d.
1.	Morning and Evening Prayer, with Responses (Ferial and Festal), Litany, and Chants for the Canticles. Demy 8vo, paper cover	1	0
	Ditto ditto ditto ditto cloth	1	6
2.	The Office of the Holy Communion, complete, with Merbecke's music. Demy 8vo, paper cover	0	8
3.	The Order of Confirmation, the Form of Solemnization of Matrimony, and the Order for the Burial of the Dead, with the necessary music. Demy 8vo, paper cover	0	8
4.	The Psalter, with Canticles and Proper Psalms, set to appropriate Chants. Demy 8vo, cloth	3	0
5.	Ditto ditto ditto. With Morning and Evening Prayer, &c. Demy 8vo, cloth	4	0
6.	The Psalter, with Canticles and Proper Psalms, pointed for Chanting. Cloth, 32mo	1	6
6A.	Ditto ditto ditto, together with Morning and Evening Prayer, with the music for the Ferial and Festal Responses, and Litany. Cloth, 32mo	2	6

TONIC SOL-FA EDITIONS.

No.		s.	d.
7.	Morning and Evening Prayer, with Responses (Ferial and Festal), Litany, and Chants for the Canticles. Demy 8vo, paper cover	1	0
	Ditto ditto ditto ditto cloth	1	6
8.	The Office of the Holy Communion, complete, with Merbecke's music. Demy 8vo, paper cover	0	8
9.	The Order of Confirmation, the Form of Solemnization of Matrimony, and the Order for the Burial of the Dead, with the necessary music. Demy 8vo, paper cover	0	8
10.	The Psalter, with Canticles and Proper Psalms, set to appropriate Chants. Demy 8vo, cloth	3	0
11.	Ditto ditto ditto. With Morning and Evening Prayer, &c. Demy 8vo, cloth	4	0
12.	The Psalter, with Canticles and Proper Psalms, pointed for Chanting, together with Morning and Evening Prayer, with the music for the Ferial and Festal Responses, and Litany. Cloth, 32mo	2	6

LONDON: NOVELLO AND COMPANY, LIMITED

(July, 1923.)

THE
NEW CATHEDRAL PSALTER

EDITED AND POINTED FOR CHANTING

BY

COSMO GORDON LANG, D.D.
(ARCHBISHOP OF YORK).

HENRY SCOTT HOLLAND, D.Litt.
(CANON AND PRECENTOR OF ST. PAUL'S)

CHARLES H. LLOYD, M.A., Mus.D.
(PRECENTOR OF ETON).

GEORGE C. MARTIN, Mus.D.
(ORGANIST OF ST. PAUL'S).

WORDS ONLY.

				Cloth. s. d.	Red Basil s. d.
No. 51.	With Superimposed notes.	Demy 8vo	.. ..	4 0	7 0
No. 61.	With Prosody signs.	Imperial 32mo		1 6	3 0
No. 62.	Ditto	Demy 8vo (large type)		4 0	7 0
No. 71.	With Varied type.	Imperial 32mo		1 6	3 0
No. 72.	Ditto	Demy 8vo		4 0	7 0

CHANTS ONLY.

				Paper. s. d.	Cloth. s. d.	Red Basil. s. d.
No. 81.	For Cathedral use, "The St. Paul's Cathedral Chant Book," revised Edition	Foolscap 4to		2 6	3 0	4 6
No. 81A.	Ditto	ditto	.. Post 4to	4 0	4 6	7 0
No. 82.	For Parish Church use, no Treble recitation note higher than D.		Foolscap 4to	2 6	3 0	4 6
No. 82A.	Ditto	ditto	.. Post 4to	4 0	4 6	7 0
No. 83.	For Village Church use, no Treble recitation note higher than C.		Foolscap 4to	2 6	3 0	4 6
No. 83A.	Ditto	ditto	.. Post 4to	4 0	4 6	7 0

PSALTER AND CHANTS COMBINED.

						Cloth. s. d.	Red Basil s. d.
No. 53.	With Superimposed notes and Chant Book No. 81.	Demy 8vo	..	..		5 6	8 6
No. 54.	Ditto	and Chant Book No. 82.	Demy 8vo	..	..	5 6	8 6
No. 55.	Ditto	and Chant Book No. 83.	Demy 8vo	..	..	5 6	8 6
No. 63.	With Prosody signs	and Chant Book No. 81.	Demy 8vo	..	..	5 6	8 6
No. 64	Ditto	and Chant Book No. 82.	Demy 8vo	..	..	5 6	8 6
No. 65	Ditto	and Chant Book No. 83.	Demy 8vo	..	..	5 6	8 6
No. 73.	With Varied type	and Chant Book No. 81.	Demy 8vo	..	..	5 6	8 6
No. 74.	Ditto	and Chant Book No. 82.	Demy 8vo	..	..	5 6	8 6
No. 75.	Ditto	and Chant Book No. 83.	Demy 8vo	..	..	5 6	8 6

The "New Cathedral Psalter," though founded on the old Cathedral Psalter, is a distinct book, and the two cannot be used together.

London: NOVELLO AND COMPANY, Limited.

(JULY, 1923.)

THE

Cathedral Prayer Book

BEING THE

Book of Common Prayer

WITH THE MUSIC NECESSARY FOR THE USE OF
CHOIRS

TOGETHER WITH THE

CANTICLES AND PSALTER

POINTED FOR CHANTING

EDITED BY

JOHN STAINER, M.A., Mus. Doc., Oxon.

AND

WILLIAM RUSSELL, M.A., Mus. Bac., Oxon.

EXTRACT FROM EDITORS' PREFACE.

THE inconvenience and costliness of the number of separate Books usually requisite for the members of a Choir, in the performance of an ordinary Choral Service, have long pointed to the desirableness of a manual which should, as far as possible, unite under one cover all that is necessary for the choral rendering of, at least, those portions of the Church's Services which are less liable to variation.

The Music of the Versicles and Responses—Festal as well as Ferial—a Psalter and Canticles pointed for chanting, are almost indispensable for the careful and accurate rendering of a Choral Service. And yet, hitherto, it has been scarcely possible to procure these, unless in separate numbers; involving not only much additional expense, but also the disadvantage arising from the continual shifting of books during service time, which is such a hindrance to a devout participation in Divine Worship.

To remedy these evils, and to assist in promoting, as it is hoped, a more careful and reverent performance of the Divine Offices, the Cathedral Prayer Book has been compiled.

The Editors are fully aware that they are not the first to make an effort in this direction. But they believe that several circumstances have tended to favour their attempt, and ensure its success, which have been wanting in other instances.

This manual provides not only for the daily Morning and Evening Prayer, and the choral celebration of the Holy Communion, in all its completeness, but also for the whole of the occasional Offices contained in the Book of Common Prayer. A special feature of it, moreover, is that it includes an Appendix, in which are contained not only Tallis's Festival Responses and Litany, but a great deal of other additional and miscellaneous matter which it is conjectured will add greatly to its usefulness and value.

The pointing of the Psalms and Canticles is after that known as the Cathedral Psalter, edited by the Rev. S. Flood-Jones, the late Mr. James Turle, the Rev. Dr. Troutbeck, Sir John Stainer, and Mr. Joseph Barnby.

An edition can also be had in which the Cathedral Psalter Chants to the Canticles and the Psalms are included.

	EDITIONS.	NET. s. d.
1.	Demy 8vo, 628 pp., large type. With Canticles and Psalter pointed for Chanting. Cloth, red edges	9 0
	Ditto, ditto. Red basil and red edges	12 0
2.	Demy 8vo, 600 pp., large type. With Canticles and Psalter pointed, set to appropriate Chants (Cathedral Psalter Chants). Cloth, red edges ..	9 0
	Ditto, ditto. Red basil and red edges	12 0
3	Imperial 32mo, 696 pp., Pocket Edition. With Canticles and Psalter pointed for Chanting. Cloth, red edges	5 6
	Ditto, ditto. Red basil and red edges	7 6

LONDON: NOVELLO AND COMPANY, LIMITED.

(July, 1923.)

This Price List cancels all previous Lists.

All Psalters and Chant Books included in this list are now issued as net publications.

THE

CATHEDRAL PSALTER

THE PSALTER ONLY.

No.			s.	d.
2.	Imperial 32mo, with Proper Psalms ... *cloth*		1	6
2B.	Ditto, ditto *red basil and red edges*		3	0
2A.	Public School Edition ... ... *cloth*		3	0
3.	Demy 8vo, large type, with Proper Psalms... ,,		4	0
3A	Ditto, ditto, ditto, *red basil and red edges*		7	0
4.	Proper Psalms, 32mo ... ... *paper cover*		0	4
5.	Canticles, 32mo...		0	1½
5.	Ditto, 8vo		0	4
16.	Imperial 32mo (Bible version) ... ... *cloth*		1	6

CHANTS ONLY.

No.			s.	d.
8.	Post 4to ... ... *paper cover*		3	0
8A.	Ditto ... ... *red basil and red edges*		7	0
9.	Ditto ... ... *cloth*		4	6
10.	Fcap. 4to... ... ... *paper cover*		1	6
10A.	Fcap. 4to... ... .. *red basil and red edges*		4	6
11.	Ditto ... ... *cloth*		2	6
13.	Sol-fa Edition ... ... *paper cover*		1	6
13A.	Ditto ... *red basil and red edges*		4	6
14.	Ditto ... ... *cloth*		2	6

THE PSALTER AND CHANTS COMBINED.

No.			s.	d.
7.	Psalter and Canticles, with Chants, 4to ... *cloth*		7	6
7A.	Ditto ditto, ditto, *red basil and red edges*		11	6
15.	Psalter and Canticles, with Chants, demy 8vo *cloth*		4	0
15A.	Ditto, ditto, ditto, *red basil and red edges*		7	0
12.	Canticles, with Chants, 4to		0	8
	Ditto, ditto, demy 8vo (3 sets) ... each		0	6

THE CHOIRBOY'S GUIDE
TO THE
CATHEDRAL PSALTER.

NOVELLO'S MUSIC PRIMERS, No. 74.   Price ONE SHILLING.

London: NOVELLO AND COMPANY, Limited.

(Aug. 1926.)

www.ingramcontent.com/pod-product-compliance
Lightning Source LLC
Chambersburg PA
CBHW031746090426
42739CB00008B/897